A Fantastic Field Trip

by C. Truman Rogers
illustrated by Dan Bridy

PEARSON

Scott
Foresman

Editorial Offices: Glenview, Illinois • Parsippany, New Jersey • New York, New York
Sales Offices: Needham, Massachusetts • Duluth, Georgia • Glenview, Illinois
Coppell, Texas • Ontario, California • Mesa, Arizona

Every effort has been made to secure permission and provide appropriate credit for photographic material. The publisher deeply regrets any omission and pledges to correct errors called to its attention in subsequent editions.

Unless otherwise acknowledged, all photographs are the property of Scott Foresman, a division of Pearson Education.

ISBN: 0-328-13408-2

3 4 5 6 7 8 9 10 V0G1 14 13 12 11 10 09 08 07 06

CONTENTS

Chapter 1 Exciting Plans

The Science Club was doing some serious planning. Well, not the entire Science Club, just the six members who were passionate about bugs.

Emma, Jacob, Kayla, Luke, Carlos, and Lily were known as the Bug Kids. They were about to take the biggest, buggiest field trip in the history of the entire universe.

Emma had brought a newspaper story to a club meeting. It was a report about a new entomological zoo—a place all about bugs!

Since the entomological exhibit was new—it hadn't even opened yet, in fact—they couldn't find out much about it. Yet it sounded fascinating and alluring. It was something, the Bug Kids agreed, they just had to do.

The Bug Kids' journey was several hours away from Waterville, so they would have to spend the night near the zoo. Mr. Edwards, their science teacher, would go with them, but they had to do the planning. All of them had to work hard to raise money to pay for the expenses.

Since they needed more grown-ups to accompany them, Mrs. Appleby, the girls' soccer coach, volunteered to go. The teachers rented a van for the Science Club. Mr. Brand, the band teacher, heard about the trip and thought it would be fun to be the driver. Finally, they were ready to depart.

Chapter 2 Finally Leaving!

The Bug Kids were scheduled to meet after school on Thursday. The plan was to sleep over and see the exhibits on Friday and stay until late afternoon. The group was due back in Waterville by 9:00 P.M. Friday night.

Jacob and Luke were the first to arrive. Jacob brought his dad's small tape recorder and promised to be in charge of recording discussions among the group. Next, Mr. Edwards arrived along with Lily. She had a big sketchbook in which she planned to make detailed sketches of the bugs.

Carlos came next, bearing two new insect guides. Only Mrs. Appleby and Emma were missing. Emma was always tearing into class at the last moment, and just as everyone expected, Emma came racing up to the van.

The other kids looked at each other, wanting to groan. But where was Mrs. Appleby?

They couldn't leave until Mrs. Appleby got there. Finally, she arrived, having been stuck in traffic. At last they were on their way.

Almost before they knew it, the van turned off the interstate onto a smooth roadway. Mr. Edwards suggested that the kids begin discussing what they were most interested in seeing. They knew there would be a lot to look at. Jacob set up his tape recorder and started documenting the oral history of their adventure.

Chapter 3 More Worries

"I hope I didn't take a wrong turn," Mr. Brand said, pulling off the road. He had planned to go back home and return for them the next day, but Luke asked, "Why don't you just stay with us once we get there? Then we'll be able to split into three groups tomorrow."

Mr. Edwards seconded that suggestion, and Mr. Brand agreed. Now the only thing left to do was to reach their goal.

"We can't be too far now," Emma assured them. She had the map and some written directions too.

Carlos seemed thoughtful and commented, "Gee, this zoo is pretty far out in the countryside, don't you think? There's nothing around for miles and miles."

Finally they saw a small sign pointing the way toward Locust Hill, the town nearest the zoo!

Just when everyone was sure they had made a wrong turn someplace, the van reached the small town of Locust Hill. And there was their motel, the Butterfly Lodge!

It was a pleasant lodging, simple but comfortable, that had been converted from an old warehouse. And, the kids were delighted to discover, all of the rooms were named after different kinds of butterflies—swallowtail, monarch, and so on—and decorated in their colors too.

The next morning, they had a quick breakfast. Everyone was too excited to eat much because they needed to get to the zoo immediately. They set off early in their van.

Chapter 4 The Amazing Zoo

Soon they were at the gates of the zoo. There was only a large hand-painted sign at the entrance: "Remarkable Entomological Zoo" with an arrow pointing down a narrow, tree-lined drive. "Where are the buildings?" Lily wondered. All they could see was a little, round house.

A gatekeeper was waving to the van to stop. "I'm Fred," he said. "We've been expecting you. You're our first visitors. Welcome!"

The van with the Bug Kids and their chaperones parked, and everyone began walking along a narrow path through the grassy meadow, following the signs with arrows pointing the way. Soon they could hear something that sounded like machinery running, or a huge swarm of bees. *We must be getting close,* they thought. But still, there weren't any buildings in sight. "I wish I could see a building or something," Jacob said.

But soon enough they came to a low building, just one story high, with an elegant sign over a heavy red door that said "Entomological Exhibition" in gold letters. Everyone sighed with relief. Here was their objective. Here was what they had worked and planned so hard to achieve. Here was—discovery!

They decided to head toward their first choice: the butterflies. Lepidoptera Hall, as the butterfly exhibit was called, was to the left, down a long sloping walkway.

The whole zoo seemed to be built underground. Although it was mild outside, the temperature got considerably warmer as the kids made their way down the walkway. It was somewhat like going into an underground mine.

As the kids got used to the low light, they could make out the shapes of trees and hear faint sounds, like passing breezes. It was all quite wonderful, but they still hadn't seen any butterflies.

Soon they saw a clearing. It was lighter there, but there were no windows to let the sunlight in. Instead, the light came from this strange new underground world they had entered—a world unlike anything they'd ever seen before!

The group hurried toward the light. The most amazing and impossible sights greeted them. Everywhere they looked, there were gigantic butterflies. Some were as large as small cars. As they flew from bush to bush their flapping wings sent gusts of wind that nearly blew the Bug Kids off their feet!

"Wow, look at the wings!" shouted Luke. "I always wondered what the scales they're made of looked like up close!" Suddenly a voice came over a loudspeaker, gentle but audible: "Please do not make loud noises while visiting the butterflies. Listen, but do not speak. Your voices will disturb them." Then the loudspeaker was silent. So were all the Bug Kids.

"Well, we wanted to see some special insects," Lily whispered to Kayla. "And we really are!" But then the loudspeaker came on again. "Silence, please."

Lily nodded silently in the direction of the loudspeaker and placed her forefinger promisingly across her lips.

As the group made its way through the meadowland, they felt a little more comfortable and began to look more carefully at what surrounded them. "Look, over there! Pupae all over those bushes! They're as big as soccer balls!" cried out Lily, forgetting herself.

Everywhere they looked, there were giant butterflies and moths at different stages of life. There were orange and black monarchs, spotted tiger moths, woolybear caterpillar pupae, and pale cabbage moths.

Because the loudspeaker had gently
but firmly requested them to be quiet,
the group refrained from talking to
one another. Instead they watched with
wonder and listened to the swishing of
the butterflies' wings as they swooped and
soared around and above them.

Lily quietly waved the other kids over
and pointed to her notebook. She had
been sketching the different stages of a
butterfly's life in realistic detail.

Chapter 5 More Strange and Fabulous Things

At the end of the exhibit, a door led to another narrow passageway. The Bug Kids made their way along the corridor until they reached a door that would not budge. A voice on the loudspeaker announced, "The next door will not open until earphones are firmly in place."

Emma hesitated. "Do we have to?" she whispered to Jacob.

"Yes!" replied the loudspeaker voice with a startling boom.

With that announcement, everyone put on earphones. "No wonder we need to wear them," Kayla said when she got near the next door. It was almost impossible to hear anything except buzzing, whining, whirring, and chirping.

Cicadas, katydids, wasps, flies, and all the other noisy insects filled an enormous room. But, like the butterflies they had just seen earlier, every flying or crawling insect in the exhibit was super-sized.

"All the better to see them," said Carlos.

Everyone stopped to watch an adult cicada crawl out of its skin, almost like unwrapping a present.

Emma suddenly started pointing wildly to the right. "Look, look over there! Look at that wasps' nest. It's as big as a garage!"

Everyone looked where she was pointing. It was a paper nest, shaped like a jar and fastened to a tree limb. Wasps were going in and out, carrying in food for the workers to feed the developing larvae.

Kayla gasped with surprise. "Imagine what the larvae must look like!" she exclaimed.

The next room had fleas that could jump 150 feet over the corridor the visitors walked along. There were giant ladybugs chomping on leaves. There were mosquitoes just as big. When they flew near the group, their whining drowned out the buzzing of all the other insects. But for some strange reason, none of the insects seemed to want to attack the tiny humans observing them.

"I wonder whether they've been bred to avoid humans?" Jacob wondered into his tape recorder.

The kids watched as insects tasted something with their antennae before eating. They saw fly larvae eating dead bugs that had fallen to the floor.

"Yuck!" said Lily. "Ugly, white gigantic worms. And they turn into dirty old flies!" But Emma reminded her that worms clean up other dead animals.

Back in the passageway, they tried to open the next door, but it wouldn't budge.

Again the loudspeaker gave them an order. "Put on the sunglasses hanging on the wall." By now they knew better than to disobey! They opened the next door and were dazzled by brilliant light. There were thousands of enormous lightning bugs.

Then, when the group went through the final door, the loudspeaker voice said, "Thank you for coming. We hope you now feel an even greater respect for insects." Then it asked, rather surprisingly, "But what kind of report will you write when you get home?"

"What a peculiar question," Lily commented to Kayla. "Did that sound to you like the voice of Fred, the gatekeeper?"

"Could be," replied Kayla. "We haven't seen any other humans here, have we?"

It was quite a thoughtful group that climbed back into the van. There was plenty to fill a report with. But who could believe such a fantastic field trip?

Magnificent Insects

"A Fantastic Field Trip" is science fiction. Giant bugs the size of school buses do not exist. They are fiction. However, the descriptions of the insects and their life cycles are real. They are based on scientific facts.

There are more kinds of insects in the world than any other group of creatures. Insects are fascinating and useful. Some of them can seem like nuisances. We do not like to have termites eating away the wood in our houses. But they clean up dead wood in the forests. Insects, like the fly larvae, eat dead animals and waste.

Butterflies have a different life cycle from humans. They grow from an egg to a caterpillar stage, then turn into a pupa or chrysalis when they rest before becoming an adult butterfly.

We can appreciate insects for pollinating plants, bringing us beauty, noisy songs, and even mysterious lights.